A First Book of Knitting
for Children

A First Book of Knitting for Children

written by
Bonnie Gosse and Jill Allerton

with photography by
Bonnie Gosse, Dave Gosse and Bryan Anderson

Wynstones Press

Published by

Wynstones Press

Ruskin Glass Centre
Wollaston Road
Stourbridge
West Midlands DY8 4HE
England.
Telephone: +44 (0) 1384 399455
Email: info@wynstonespress.com
Website: wynstonespress.com

Second edition 2004. Reprinted 2007.
First edition 1995. Printed 4 times.

Illustrations by Vicky Croydon.

The publisher expresses thanks to the late Kay Eastmond for assistance
in the preparation of the original edition of this book.

British Library Cataloguing-in-Publication Data:
A catalogue record for this book is available from the British Library.

Printed in EU by mccgraphics.co.uk

ISBN 9780946206 55 1

Contents

Dedication	6
History of Knitting	7
Yarn	7
Tools	9
Ways to begin	10
Holding the needles	11
Casting on	12
Disappearing knot	12
Disappearing knot verse	12
Casting on verse	14
Knit stitch	18
Knit stitch verse	18
Knit stitch problems	22
Knitting the bush by mistake	23
Forgetting to knit the last stitch	23
Putting your needle in under the wrong fence	24
Knitting backwards	25
Undoing knitting	26
Undoing a stitch	26
Undoing stitches verse	26
Undoing a row	28
Recovering a dropped stitch	29
Slipped stitches	31
Shaping your knitting by decreasing	32
Changing colours	33
Casting off	35
Casting off verse	35
Finger knitting	38
Sewing up projects	40
Stuffing projects	40

Projects using knit stitch only	41
Striped ball	42
Lamb	44
Lion	47
Pig	52
Elephant	56
Doll	60
Horse	64
Purl stitch	70
Purl stitch verse	70
Stocking stitch	73
Ribbing	74
Purl stitch problems	75
A mistake in stocking stitch	75
Mistakes in ribbing	75
Projects using knit stitch and purl stitch	77
Cat	78
Chicken	80
Making a pom-pom	82
Mother Sea Otter	83
Boy with hands in his pockets	87
Girl with hands in her pockets	90
Making your own wooden knitting needles	91
Bibliography	93
By the same authors	94
Biographies	95

Dedication

For Lindsay Gordon
and her family

History of Knitting

For many hundreds of years people have made knitted clothing to either keep themselves warm or to make themselves beautiful. The way that we knit today, using two needles, was probably started by ancient Arab peoples. They probably used needles of bone, ivory or copper wire. Missionaries and traders spread this craft from the Middle East to Europe and Asia. It was mostly men – shepherds, fishermen and soldiers – who knitted at this time. Soon both men and women were knitting clothing for themselves or knitting as a way to earn money. Then there were many groups of knitters who fashioned very beautiful and expensive pieces of clothing, or other articles, for sale to either rich people or kings. When the knitting machine was invented hand knitting as a trade gradually died out, but people still knitted for themselves and their families.

Today, most of the hand knitting in North America and Europe is done by women. It is still as popular as it was many years ago. Standard size needles, patterns, and a great variety of styles and colours of yarn make hand knitting today an easy, exciting craft.

Yarn

Yarn is made by spinning (twisting) fibres together to make a long thin thread. The long thin thread is called a ply. Two, three, four or more plys are then twisted together to make the yarn.

People use many different kinds of fibres to make yarn:
- wool from animals: sheep, dogs, goats, rabbits, yaks, llamas, camels;
- fibres from plants: cotton, flax, hemp;
- fibres from insects: silk;
- synthetic fibres: people have made yarn from many different products that you would never think they could make yarn from. For example, wood, glass, petroleum, metal, and the protein from some foods such as milk, corn and peanuts.

There are different good things about each type of fibre. We have used yarn that is

Yarn

made of wool from sheep to knit all the projects in this book because we like the way it feels and looks.

Yarn is sold in balls or skeins. The label on the yarn will tell you all about the yarn: the fibre used in the yarn, the thickness of the yarn, how much the yarn weighs, and how to care for a garment made from this yarn. It is confusing because there are so many different types of yarns to choose from! If we are not sure about the yarn to use, we ask for help at the yarn store so that we choose a yarn that is the most suitable for the project that we wish to knit.

If the yarn comes in a skein you need to wind it into a ball so it doesn't become tangled when you are using it.

1) Untwist the yarn

2) Place the yarn over the backs of two chairs.

3) Undo the knots in the ends or cut the yarn ties around the skein.

4) Take one of the loose ends and wind it around your fingers about 15 times.

5) Take the loops of yarn off your fingers and keep wrapping the yarn around these first loops to form a ball.

Walk around the chairs as you wind the yarn into a ball. Wrap the yarn gently because if you pull it too tightly it will stretch and lose its elastic quality. Keep turning the ball as you wind the yarn onto it.

Tools

Needles

Today, needles are usually made from plastic, aluminium, wood or bamboo. They come in different lengths and thicknesses. Some needles have points on one end and knobs on the other end. These are sold 2 needles together. Needles with points at both ends are sold 4 or 5 together. You usually use thicker needles with thicker yarn and thinner needles with thinner yarn. You can tell the thickness of the needles by looking at the number on the knob at the end of the needle or at the number on the package.

The same standard sized needles are sold in all countries of the world, but in different countries people call them by different names. For example, in Canada we use millimetres to measure the size of needles, and all the projects in this book have been made using either 6mm or 4mm sized needles. However, in the United States these same needles are called size 10 and size 5, and in the United Kingdom they are called size 4 and size 8. You can buy a needle gauge to show the thickness of a needle, and tell you the size in any of the three different ways for naming the thicknesses of needles.

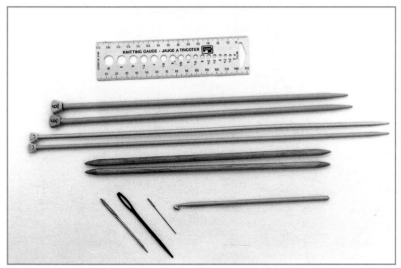

Top to bottom: needle guage; 6mm needles; 4mm needles; 6mm needles with points on both ends; crochet hook; wool needle, plastic bodkin and tapestry needle.

Tools

Crochet hook

This is useful for picking up dropped stitches and for putting on trim. Use a crochet hook of medium size.

Sewing up needles

You will need a needle for sewing up your projects. A wool needle or tapestry needle is easy to use with a lighter weight yarn, as these have large eyes and blunt points. But when you are working with a thicker yarn you will need a needle with an even larger eye than these two needles. You will need a bodkin. Either a metal or a plastic bodkin will be fine.

Ways to begin

You use both of your hands to knit. Each hand does something different but both are equally active. Because of this we give only one set of instructions for 'knitting'. Even if you write or draw with your left hand follow these instructions. You will knit in exactly the same way as someone who writes or draws with their right hand.

To help you learn and remember each of the steps or stitches in 'knitting' we have used short 'picture' verses for the instructions. Each step or stitch will have its own verse and set of photographs. It is, of course, much easier to be taught a subject by another person than to teach oneself from a book, because the teacher can answer questions and help with difficulties as they arise. We have included answers to many different questions and problems which may arise as you learn to knit, but should difficulties persist, we must recommend asking a friend or family member for assistance.

Holding the needles

There are many different ways to hold knitting needles. We find the easiest way is to perch with your hands above the needles.

You always hold the needle with the stitches on it in your left hand, with the empty needle in your right hand. You use your right hand to move the yarn. You will make new stitches from the stitches on your left hand needle as you move these stitches over to your right hand needle.

Casting on

Disappearing knot

Putting the first row of stitches on the knitting needle is called casting on. To begin with you make a 'disappearing knot'. This knot is called disappearing because if you pull its short end, it just disappears.

Disappearing knot verse

Around two fingers,
Over the yarn,
Pull a loop through,
Jump out of the barn.

Around two fingers,

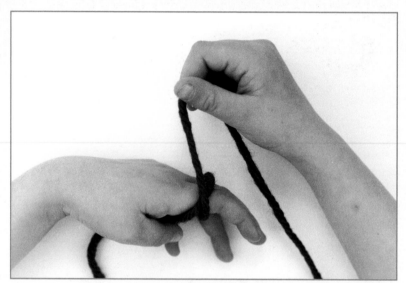

Over the yarn,

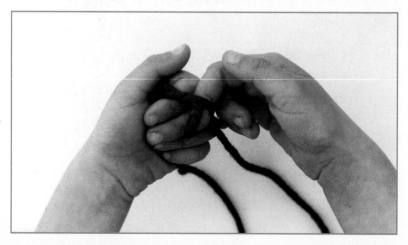

Casting on

Pull a loop through,

Jump out of the barn.

13

Casting on

Put the disappearing knot on your left hand needle. Now you will use both needles to put your stitches on your left hand needle beside the disappearing knot. We like to think of putting birdies on a branch.

Casting on verse

In through the front door,
Dance around the back,
Peek through the window,
And on jumps Jack.

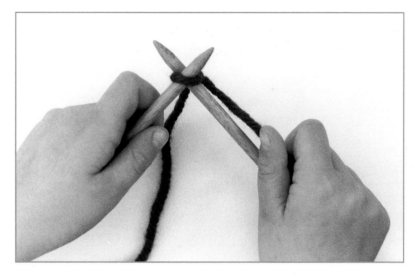

In through the front door,

Dance around the back,

Casting on

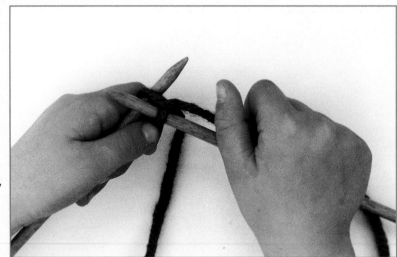

Peek through the window,

(You are bringing a
new loop of yarn back
through the front door)

And on jumps Jack.

Casting on

Two stitches cast on the needle (the right hand needle is in the front door again ready to cast on another stitch).

One row (8 stitches) cast on the needle.

17

Knit stitch

Now you are ready to start knitting. There are two basic stitches in knitting, a knit stitch and a purl stitch. We will start with a knit stitch.

Remember, you hold your needle with the stitches on it in your left hand and the empty needle in your right hand. You will use your right hand to move the yarn. You will make new stitches from the stitches on your left hand needle as you move those stitches over to your right hand needle.

Knit stitch verse

Under the fence,
Catch the sheep,
Back we come,
Off we leap.

Under the fence,

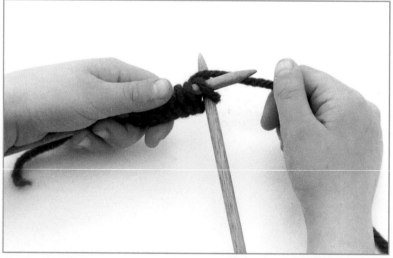

Catch the sheep,

Knit stitch

Back we come,

This is a tricky part as sometimes you come back and lose
your sheep on the way.
You will find it easier to keep
your sheep on the needle if
you keep holding onto the
yarn so it is snug around
the needle.

As you bring this new loop of
yarn forward, under your left
hand needle and through the
old stitch on the left hand
needle, you are making a new
stitch on your right hand
needle.

Off we leap.

Knit stitch

When you have finished the row, all the stitches will be on your right hand needle and the yarn will be coming out of the very last stitch.

Turn your knitting around. Put it in your left hand and you are ready to start the next row. When starting the new row, be careful to use the yarn coming from the ball, and not Lily's tail, which will not take you very far!

Keep knitting row after row. You will see rows of bumps on both the front and reverse sides of your knitting. This is happening because when you knit a stitch a bump is made on the back of the stitch, that is the side away from you. This type of pattern that has rows of bumps on both sides is called garter stitch. We wondered if this is because it resembles garter snakes lying side by side!

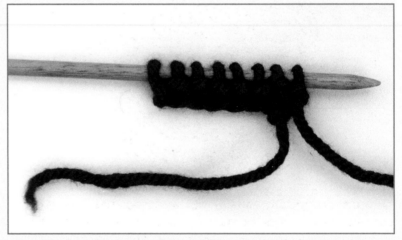

This shows one finished row of knitting. It has been turned around to show the side that was away from you when you knitted it. Each bump is the back of one knit stitch.
The short piece of yarn hanging down is 'Lily's tail'.

You are now ready to start on your first project, and your learning can continue while you work on this. The striped ball on page 42 is really easy to knit and either lots of fun to play with or to give as a gift.

You will need to read the next section, Knit stitch problems – where they occur and how to correct them, and later you will need to know how to change colours, page 33, casting off, page 35 and sewing up, page 40.

This picture shows 12 rows of knitting completed (6 rows of bumps or 6 wavy lines, because it takes two rows of knitting to make one row of bumps). Don't count the straight row of bumps at the beginning - this is the casting on row.

Knit stitch problems –
where they occur and how to correct them

The first stitch in a row is often the most difficult, because it is sometimes hard to tell where to go in under the fence. You need to pull the bush (the last stitch on the last row that you have just completed) down out of the way so that you can see exactly where to go in under the fence. If you go under the bush as well as under the fence, you will be making an extra stitch and your knitting will become wider and wider.

Here the bush is hiding the way to go in under the fence.

Here the bush is pulled down so that you can see where to go in under the fence.

This knitting is becoming wider because the knitter has knitted the bush at the beginning of each row.

Can you see the yarn coming from the second stitch instead of the first?

Knitting the bush by mistake

To correct this problem of your knitting becoming wider, because you have been going in under the bush at the beginning of each row, you will need to undo your knitting row by row back to before you made the mistake. Undoing knitting is demonstrated on pages 26 to 28.

Forgetting to knit the last stitch

Sometimes you think that the row is completed but the very last stitch has not been knitted. When you turn your knitting around to start the next row, you will see the yarn coming out of the second stitch instead of the first.

To correct this, turn your knitting around again, slip the unknit stitch back onto your left hand needle, and knit this stitch as normal.

Knit stitch problems

Putting your needle in under the wrong fence

Occasionally when you are knitting a row, you put your needle in the wrong place – you go in under the wrong fence. If you put your needle in under the yarn that is between the needles, and then knit this, you will be adding more stitches and making holes in your knitting.

Can you see the hole and the extra stitch made by putting the needle into the wrong place?

To correct this type of hole and extra stitches in your knitting, you need to undo your knitting to a point before you made the mistake – instructions on pages 26 to 28.

If you have been making this mistake often, you need to watch carefully where you put your needle each time you start a stitch.

Knit stitch problems

Knitting backwards

Sometimes when you are knitting it is necessary to put it down for a while when you are in the middle of a row.

When you come back again, remember that the needle with more rows of knitting on it and with the yarn coming out of its last stitch goes in your right hand. Remember, you are making new stitches as you move the stitches from your left, to the right hand needle.

This photograph shows the effect of having knitted in the wrong direction after forgetting which way to start again in the middle of a row. We call it going the wrong way to market. You will see that there is an extra row of bumps part way through the knitting.

Undoing knitting

There are two different ways to undo knitting. The first is to undo it stitch by stitch.
You use this when there are only a few stitches a little way back to correct. The second
way is to undo your knitting a row at a time. You use this when you either have to go back
a long way to reach a mistake, or if there are many corrections to do.

Undoing a stitch

Undoing stitches verse
In through the basement,
Pull out the stick,
Free flies the yarn.

In through the basement,
(using your left hand
needle)

Pull out the stick,
(this is your right hand
needle)

Free flies the yarn.

Undoing a row

To undo by the row you pull out the needle, leaving all the loops standing up free. You then very gently pull the yarn. This may make you feel nervous, because all the stitches just pull out. You must be very careful at the end of the row, that you do not start pulling the next row, unless this is your intention. This method may be used to undo many rows at a time if necessary.

Now you have to put all the stitches back onto the needle. There are two things which require particular attention. Place your knitting with the yarn to the right, and insert the needle into the stitches from left to right as in the photo. You must try to put all your stitches facing the same way onto your needle.

When you come to knit the next row, if a stitch is not facing the right way, slip it off the left hand needle, turn the stitch around and put it back on the left hand needle.

Recovering a dropped stitch

Sometimes when you are knitting you drop a stitch, that is, a stitch comes undone all by itself, and you have a loop and a separate bar of yarn just hanging loose. If this has happened just one row down it is easy to fix. Move the stitches on your needles until the dropped stitch is in between your two needles – you might have to undo some stitches.

Put your crochet hook through the dropped stitch. Hook the bar of yarn and pull it through to make the new stitch. Put this stitch onto your left hand needle.

The only problem which may occur is picking up the stitch from the wrong side. If you do

Recovering a dropped stitch

this, then your row of bumps will have one smooth stitch in it where you picked up the stitch. To remedy this, just undo the one stitch again, turn your knitting around, and put the loop on the other side of the straight piece of yarn and pick the stitch up this way.

It is possible to pick up dropped stitches from many rows down if necessary. In garter stitch knitting – where you knit each row – if you are picking up stitches from many rows down, you must keep turning your knitting around with each stitch picked up, so that the bumps will always be on the correct side. This is very difficult, and a beginner will often need assistance from someone more experienced.

It is possible to drop a stitch and not notice it until many rows later. When you do realise the mistake, your knitting may have pulled in, making it very difficult to pick up the dropped stitch. One remedy for this is to sew the little loop of the dropped stitch to the stitches on either side, to prevent it dropping further. Use the same coloured thread as your yarn so it does not show.

Can you see the little loop of the dropped stitch? Can you see that there is one stitch fewer on the needle?

Slipped stitches

Sometimes when you are doing a knit stitch you don't bring the sheep back properly. It slips unknitted off your left hand needle and onto your right hand one, and it feels as if you have really knitted it.

When you first start knitting you will have to watch every move you make with your needles.

If you slip a stitch, you will see later in your knitting a little loose bar of yarn hanging out at this point. If you have many of these, then perhaps you should slow down your knitting and watch very carefully each time you bring back the sheep. Remember that if you keep holding the yarn tightly with your right hand you will find it easier to bring back the new loop of yarn – the sheep – under the fence.

If you notice that you have just slipped a stitch, you may treat it like a dropped stitch using your crochet hook to pick it up, if it is only 1 or 2 rows down. If there are many slipped stitches, you will probably find it easier to fix them by undoing your knitting row by row until all are reached.

Shaping your knitting by decreasing

Sometimes you need to make your knitting narrower – for example when you are knitting the pig's head. To do this you lose or decrease one stitch at a time by knitting two stitches together.

In through two front doors,

Dance around the back,
Peek through two windows,
And off jump two Jacks (as one stitch).

Changing colours

When you change colours of yarn one side of your knitting will have a change mark – see the first photo on page 34 showing the wrong side when changing colours. You usually change your yarn so that this mark shows on the back, or wrong side, of your knitting. If you want all the change marks on the wrong side of your knitting then follow these instructions.

Change the colour when the right side of your knitting is facing you and you are ready to start a new row.

Cut off the old yarn. Tie the new yarn on. Knit as usual.

Changing colours

Back, or wrong side.

Front, or right side.

Casting off

Casting off is taking stitches off your needles. You use this when you have either finished your knitting or when you wish to make your knitting narrower.

Casting off verse

To begin:
  Knit yourself over,
And continue:
  Invite a friend too,
  Leap frog over,
  Lie down Sue.

Knit yourself over,

35

Casting off

Invite a friend too,

Leap frog over,
Lie down Sue.

When you leap frog over your friend you jump right off the end of the right hand needle and lie down.

Casting off

You can count how many stitches have leap frogged off the needle because you can see them lying down. Here 4 stitches have been cast off and are lying down.

When you have only the last stitch left on the needle, pull the needle out, cut the yarn and put the rabbit in the hole. Pull the yarn snug and you have finished casting off.

Finger Knitting

Finger knitting is very useful for making tails for your projects, though you can use it for many other things too. You can use one, two or more pieces of yarn when you finger knit, depending on how thick you want the finished finger knitting to be.

Make a disappearing knot. Leave a piece of yarn about the length of your hand at the end so you will have lots of yarn to attach the finger knitting to your project. If you are using two or more pieces of yarn treat them just as if they are one piece of yarn.

Hold the end piece of yarn of the disappearing knot in your left hand.

Reach through the disappearing knot with your right hand.

Pull a loop of yarn back through the disappearing knot. This will make a new disappearing knot. As you pull this loop through, the first disappearing knot tightens up into a stitch.

You just keep reaching through the last disappearing knot and pulling back a new loop to make a new disappearing knot.

Sometimes the loop in the disappearing knot gets too large to handle easily, or the lake gets too large to fish in. It is much easier to catch a fish in a small lake. When this happens, just pull the piece

Go fishing in the lake,

Hold on tight as you pull your fish out,

Wow! The fish turns into a new lake.

of yarn which comes from the ball of yarn, to make the loop of the disappearing knot smaller.

To finish off a chain of finger knitting, cut the yarn that is coming from the ball so you have a hand length of yarn. Put this piece of yarn in the disappearing loop and gently pull it tight.

Sewing up projects

There are two methods of sewing up projects. You may sew up with the right-sides together and then turn the project right side out; the striped ball is the only project in this book for which we have used this method of sewing up. The alternative method is to sew together with the right-sides out. This is the method we prefer as it is easier and the results are better, but you do need to be neat and careful when sewing up as your stitches will show.

Use the same colour yarn as you were knitting with, so your sewing shows as little as possible. Use either a blunt-ended wool or tapestry needle.

Start with a knot in the end of the yarn. Hold the 2 edges together that you wish to sew. Sometimes you need to pin the edges together because it is too difficult to both hold and sew them simultaneously. Go through and over the first stitch on each piece. Tuck the knot into the inside. Keep doing this all the way along the edge of your knitting – this is called oversewing. Complete each seam with a locking stitch. A locking stitch is three stitches all on top of each other with the needle going through the loop of the last stitch.

Sew up your other seams but leave a little hole so that you can stuff your project, to be finally sewn up after stuffing.

Stuffing projects

You can use all sorts of materials to stuff your projects. We really like to use unspun, washed sheep's wool (it is called wool fleece) because it feels and smells so nice. You can use polyester stuffing that you buy in bags from a yarn or craft store. Old cut up sweaters or socks or panty hose work well. Odd pieces of wool or material will also do.

The final shape and appearance of your project will depend very much on the stuffing. You will need to use your hands both during and after stuffing to mould and shape your project, particularly with the more complicated animals.

Projects using knit stitch only

These projects use only casting on, knit stitch and casting off. They are a little easier than the projects in the following section which use the purl stitch also.

Most of the projects in this first section are shown using 6mm (US g10) needles and 'chunky' weight yarn. It is easier to start knitting with thicker needles and heavier yarn than with thinner needles and lighter yarn, because it is easier to see your stitches. All of these first projects that are shown using the thicker needles and heavier yarn can also be knitted with the thinner needles and lighter yarn, in which case they will, of course, be smaller. When a more finely knitted project is required, we have used 'double knitting' weight yarn with 4mm (US g6) needles.

Striped ball

6mm (US g10) needles, small quantities of various colours of 'chunky' weight yarn, fleece for stuffing, sewing up needle or bodkin.

Cast on 16 stitches.

Knit 48 rows (**24 rows of bumps on the front**).

Change the colour of the yarn whenever you wish. Remember if you want the change marks to be on the wrong side, then change the colour when the right side of your knitting is facing you, and you are ready to start a new row.

Cast off all your stitches.

Sewing up

Put the casting on edge and casting off edge together, with the right side on the inside, and all the ends of the yarn on your left.

Make a knot and start at the right hand end of the seam that you are sewing up. Sew over and over the two edges together. This is called oversewing.

Make a locking stitch at the other end.

Do not cut this yarn yet, as you use it for the next step, which is gathering one end and pulling it together. To do this, put your needle and yarn in and out of the loops all the way around the

48 rows

16 stitches

42

edge of your knitting. When you are back to where you started, gently pull the yarn so you pull your knitting into a tight circle with no hole in it.

Make a firm locking stitch and cut the yarn.

Turn your ball right side out so that all the ends of yarn are inside.

Stuff with fleece so the ball is really firm and round.

With a new piece of yarn go in and out the loops, like you did at the other end.

Pull up as before and secure with a firm locking stitch.

43

Lamb

6mm (US g10) needles, 2 balls 50 gram 'chunky' weight yarn, fleece for stuffing, sewing up needle or bodkin.

(This lamb can be made smaller by using thinner needles and thinner yarn).

You start knitting at the lamb's back legs and behind.

Cast on 36 stitches.

Knit 10 rows (5 rows of bumps on the front). This forms the back legs.

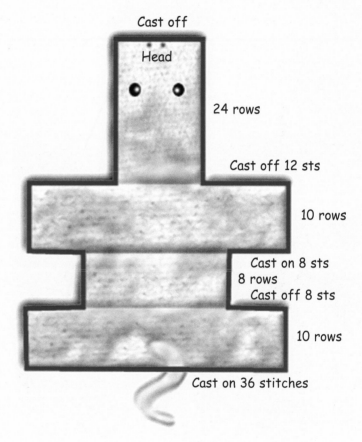

Lamb

At the beginning of each of the next 2 rows cast off 8 stitches. You should have 20 stitches remaining on your needle. This completes the back legs.

Knit 8 rows (4 rows of bumps on the front). This forms the tummy area.

At the beginning of each of the next two rows cast on 8 stitches.
You should have 36 stitches on your needle. These are the first edges of the front legs.

Casting on at the beginning of a knitted row is easy. You do exactly the same movements as when you begin to cast on.

Knit 10 rows (5 rows of bumps on the front). This forms the front legs.

At the beginning of each of the next two rows cast off 12 stitches.
This is the second edge of the front legs. You should have 12 stitches remaining on your needle.

Knit 24 rows (12 rows of bumps on the front). This forms the head.

Cast off.

Cast off

Head

24 rows

Cast off 12 sts

10 rows

Cast on 8 sts
8 rows
Cast off 8 sts

10 rows

Cast on 36 stitches

Lamb

Sewing up

LEGS: Sew the legs first. Fold each in half lengthwise so the leg will be long and thin. Sew across the end and up the leg.

Stuff all four legs. Make sure they are nice and firm.

BODY: Now fold the lamb in half and sew from his behind down under his tummy to the front legs. Stuff the behind and tummy.

HEAD: To shape the head, fold the head in half so it is long and thin.

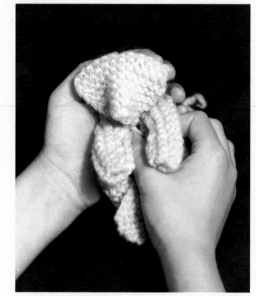

The cast off edge will be folded in half. Sew across the top of the head (along the cast off edge). Now fold this sewn-up edge down to meet where the front legs come together. Sew the two side seams of the head and the little tiny neck.

Stuff the head, the neck and between the front legs. Finish sewing up this last seam.

You can add eyes and a finger knitted collar if you like.

TAIL: Finger knit a tail and sew it on.

Use your hands to mould and shape your lamb.

Here the head has been folded down. Can you see the little side seams on the head that you need to sew up?

Lion

6mm (US g10) needles, 2 balls 50 gram 'chunky' weight yarn, fleece for stuffing, thin thread for eyes, sewing up needle or bodkin.

(This lion can be made smaller by using thinner needles and thinner yarn).

You knit the whole of the lion in one piece.

Start knitting at the lion's face.

Cast on 16 stitches.

Knit 14 rows (7 rows of bumps). This forms the head.

At the beginning of each of the next 2 rows cast on 10 stitches. These are the first edges of the front legs, and you will now have 36 stitches on your needle.

Knit 16 rows (8 rows of bumps) across these 36 stitches. This forms the front legs at each side of the body.

At the beginning of each of the next 2 rows cast off 7 stitches. You should have 22 stitches remaining on your needle. This completes the front legs.

Knit 14 rows (7 rows of bumps) across these 22 stitches. This is the tummy area.

Lion

Now divide the stitches in half to make the 2 back legs:

Knit 11 stitches, then slip the last 11 stitches, without knitting them, from your left hand needle to a very large safety pin. Close the safety pin so these 11 stitches will be safe while you knit the first 11 stitches for the first back leg.

Knit 17 rows (9 rows of bumps altogether, because you have already knitted 1 row of this leg).

Cast off.

Put the stitches from the safety pin onto your needle. Make sure that you have the point of the needle facing towards the centre of the lion. You have to start with a new piece of yarn which you tie on to the first stitch.

Knit 18 rows (9 rows of bumps). This forms the second back leg.

Cast off.

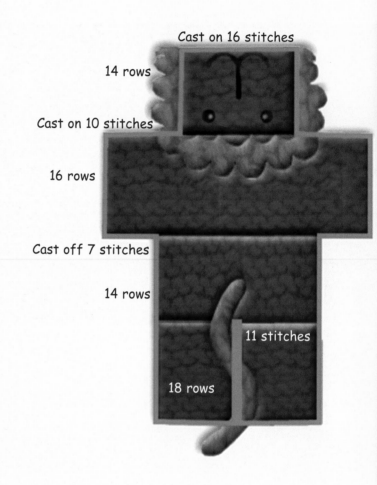

Cast on 16 stitches

14 rows

Cast on 10 stitches

16 rows

Cast off 7 stitches

14 rows

11 stitches

18 rows

Lion

Sewing up

The sewing up of the lion may be a little bit tricky – follow the instructions carefully!

Fold your piece of knitting in half lengthwise, so you can see the outline of your lion.

BACK LEGS: Sew the back legs up first. Fold one back leg in half lengthwise so the leg will be long and skinny. Make small in and out stitches along the cast off edge (the bottom of the foot). Gently pull this in so it forms a small circle.

Sew up the inside seam of the leg, using small stitches so the leg will not stretch out of shape. Sew the second back leg up in the same way.

Stuff the back legs.

BODY: Sew the body seam from the back legs to the front legs.

Stuff the body. This is the tricky part, as the legs will be sticking straight out as if your lion has had a terrible fright!

You need to stuff your lion's behind quite full of stuffing. Push and mould the behind until it has a nice round shape. Keep pulling the legs down to help shape the behind.

FRONT LEGS: Sew the front legs. Fold them lengthwise, just as you did for the back legs. Go in and out with small stitches, pulling the yarn in to make rounded paws, then sew up the inside seam.

Stuff the front legs.

Sew up the seam between the front legs.

HEAD: Fold the head in half lengthwise so it is long and skinny. Sew the neck and head seam up to the cast on edge.

Stuff the neck and head.

Make small in and out stitches along the cast on edge and pull up into a circle to form the nose.

Use your hands to shape the head properly.

Your lion will look a little strange until you get his mane on!

ADDING THE LION'S MANE: You can use either the same or a differently coloured yarn for your lion's mane. Take a long piece of yarn, thread it into your sewing up needle, and pull the ends together to make it double.

Now use loop and lock stitches, as follows:

Find the sixth bumpy row from the lion's nose.

Locking stitch: Make a regular stitch but don't pull it tight, leave a little loop: put your needle through this loop, then pull the stitch tight.

Loop stitch: Make a loop about the length of your little finger, stitch into your lion and out again, near your locking stitch. Do another locking stitch.

Keep going all the way around your lion's head.

Make a second row of the mane along the seventh bumpy row from the nose.

EARS and TAIL: Finger knit ears and tail (see page 38 for notes on finger knitting).

EARS: Finger knit two ears about eight stitches long. Leave long ends on both ends of the finger knitting and use these ends to sew the ears on in front of the mane.

TAIL: Use two strands of yarn together to finger knit the tail. Sew it on in the right place.

If you like, you can use a thin yarn or embroidery thread to give your lion two eyes and a mouth.

Pig

4mm (US g6) needles, 1 ball 50 gram 'double knitting' weight yarn, fleece for stuffing, thin thread for eyes, sewing up needle or bodkin.

(This pig can be made bigger by using thicker needles and thicker yarn).

You start knitting at the pig's back legs and behind.

Cast on 37 stitches.

Knit 12 rows (6 rows of bumps). This forms the back legs.

At the beginning of each of the next 2 rows cast off 5 stitches.
This completes the back legs. You should now have 27 stitches remaining on your needle.

Knit 12 rows (6 rows of bumps). This is the tummy area.

At the beginning of each of the next 2 rows cast on 5 stitches. These are the first edges of the front legs. You should now have 37 stitches on your needle.

Knit 12 rows (6 rows of bumps). This forms the front legs.

At the beginning of the next 2 rows cast off 7 stitches. This completes the front legs. You should now have 23 stitches remaining on your needle.

Knit 2 rows (1 row of bumps). This is the neck.

HEAD: Decrease for the head as follows:

First row: Knit 9, knit 2 stitches together, knit 1, knit 2 stitches together, knit 9.

Remember, when knitting 2 stitches together, you go under the 2 fences at the same time and treat it as if you have just gone under one fence.

Second row: Knit 8, knit 2 stitches together, knit 1, knit 2 stitches together, knit 8.

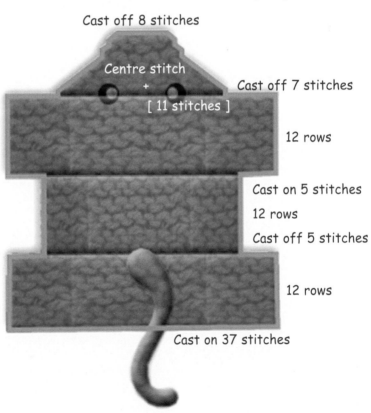

Cast off 8 stitches

Centre stitch
+
[11 stitches]

Cast off 7 stitches

12 rows

Cast on 5 stitches

12 rows

Cast off 5 stitches

12 rows

Cast on 37 stitches

Pig

Third row: Knit 7, knit 2 stitches together, knit 1, knit 2 stitches together, knit 7.

Fourth row: Knit 6, knit 2 stitches together, knit 1, knit 2 stitches together, knit 6.

Fifth row: Knit 5, knit 2 stitches together, knit 1, knit 2 stitches together, knit 5.

Sixth row: Knit 4, knit 2 stitches together, knit 1, knit 2 stitches together, knit 4.
You should now have 11 stitches remaining on your needle.

Knit 1 row without decreasing.

Knit 3, knit 2 stitches together, knit 1, knit 2 stitches together, knit 3.

Knit 1 row without decreasing.

Knit 2, knit 2 stitches together, knit 1, knit 2 stitches together, knit 2.
You should now have 7 stitches remaining on your needle.

Cast off.

EARS:

Cast on 5 stitches.

Knit 9 rows.

In each of the next 3 rows knit the second and third stitches together so you are decreasing one stitch each row. **Finally, you should now have 2 stitches remaining on your needle.**

Cast off.

2 stitches cast off

3 rows

9 rows

Cast on 5 stitches

Sewing up

LEGS: Sew up the legs first. Fold the first leg lengthwise so it is long and skinny. Sew across the end and up the leg. Sew the other legs the same way. Stuff each leg so they are all nice and firm.

BODY and HEAD: Fold the pig in half lengthwise. Sew from the nose to the back legs. Stuff and shape. Make some eyes with thin thread.

Sew the remainder of the body from the back legs to the behind. When you are shaping the pig's behind, you sew about halfway up and then tuck the last piece of knitting in and sew it to make a rounded shape.

EARS: Sew the ears on so that they hang down.

TAIL: Finger knit a tail and sew it on.

EYES: Use thin thread to make the eyes.

Elephant

6mm (US g10) needles, 2 balls 50 gram 'chunky' weight yarn, fleece for stuffing, thin thread for eyes, sewing up needle or bodkin.

(This elephant can be made smaller by using thinner needles and thinner yarn).

You start knitting at the elephant's back legs and behind.

Cast on 36 stitches.

Knit 18 rows (9 rows of bumps). This forms the back legs.

At the beginning of each of the next 2 rows cast off 9 stitches.
This completes the back legs. You should now have 18 stitches remaining on your needle.

Knit 8 rows
(4 rows of bumps).
This forms the tummy area.

At the beginning of each
of the next 2 rows cast on
9 stitches.
These are the first edges of the front
legs.

Knit 18 rows
(8 rows of bumps).
This forms the front legs.

At the beginning of each
of the next 2 rows cast off
9 stitches.
This completes the front legs. You
should now have 18 stitches remaining
on your needle.

Knit 14 rows
(7 rows of bumps).
This forms the neck and head.

At the beginning of each
the next 10 rows decrease
1 stitch. To decrease 1 stitch you knit
the first 2 stitches together just as if
they were only one stitch – you put
your needle under two fences at the
same time. You should now have only 8
stitches left on your needle.

Knit 14 rows
(7 rows of bumps).
This forms the trunk.

Cast off.

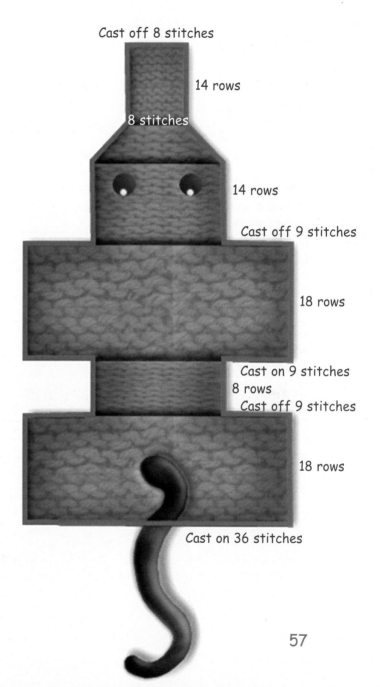

Cast off 8 stitches

14 rows

8 stitches

14 rows

Cast off 9 stitches

18 rows

Cast on 9 stitches
8 rows
Cast off 9 stitches

18 rows

Cast on 36 stitches

Elephant

EARS:

Cast on 10 stitches.

Knit 14 rows (7 rows of bumps).

Cast off, leaving a long end.

Using your bodkin, take this long piece of yarn and make small in and out stitches around three sides of the ear. Gently pull this yarn a little tighter so the ear becomes slightly rounded.

Ears

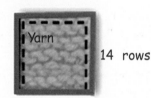

14 rows

Cast on 10 stitches

Rounded shape after pulling yarn tighter

Sewing up

LEGS: Sew the legs up first. Fold each leg in half lengthwise so it will be long, and sew across the end and up the leg. Sew the other legs the same way.

Stuff all four legs. Make sure they are nice and firm.

BODY: Now fold the elephant in half lengthwise and sew from his behind down under his tummy to just beyond the front legs. When you are sewing the elephant's behind, you sew about halfway down then fold the corner in a little and go back and sew it again. This is so his behind will be rounded instead of square. We imagine that it makes it more comfortable for him to sit.

Stuff the body firmly.

TRUNK and HEAD: Fold the trunk and head in half lengthwise. Sew from the chest to the beginning of the trunk, stuffing as you go. After each sewing stitch pull the yarn very tight. This will pull the head down into a natural pose. Continue to sew the length of the trunk leaving the end open, so he can use the tip of his trunk to pick up food or give himself a bath. Don't stuff the trunk.

EARS: Now, putting the flat edge of the ear next to the body, sew the ear on in the right place.

TAIL: Make a finger knitted tail and sew it on in the right place.

Doll

4mm (US g6) needles, 1 ball 50 gram 'double knitting' weight yarn, fleece for stuffing, sewing up needle or bodkin, light coloured t-shirt material for the head and hands, sewing needle and light coloured thread, coloured fleece for the hair, embroidery thread or coloured pens for the eyes and mouth.

(This project does not work well with thicker needles and yarn).

You start knitting at the doll's shoulders.

Cast on 36 stitches.

Knit 12 rows (6 rows of bumps). This is the first half of each arm.

To make the neck hole: Knit 19 stitches. Cast off 2 stitches by leapfrogging stitch 18 over stitch 19. Knit stitch 20 and leapfrog stitch 19 over it. Knit 16 stitches to finish the row.

Knit 17 stitches on this next row. Right now, in the middle of this row turn your knitting around and cast on 2 stitches. Now turn your knitting back, knit the 2 new stitches and the 17 stitches remaining on this row. Knit 12 rows (6 rows of bumps). **This completes the arms.**

At the beginning of each of the next 2 rows cast off 9 stitches. **18 stitches remaining.**

At the beginning of each of the next 2 rows cast on 6 stitches. You should now have 30 stitches on your needle. This will add the extra width needed for the body and legs.

Knit 16 rows (8 rows of bumps). This forms the body of the doll.

You make the legs for the doll in the same way in which you made the legs for the lion (see page 48). Half of the stitches are used for each leg.

LEGS:

Knit 15 stitches, then slip the last 15 stitches, without knitting them, onto a big safety pin. Close the safety pin so these 15 stitches will be safe while you knit the first 15 stitches for the first leg.

Knit back and forth on the first 15 stitches:

Knit 33 rows (17 rows of bumps altogether because you have already knitted 1 row for this leg). This forms the first leg.

Cast off.

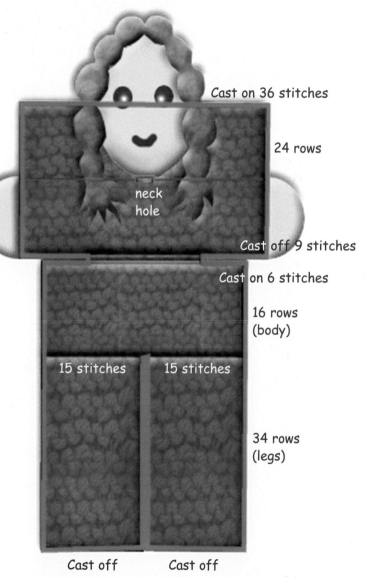

Cast on 36 stitches

24 rows

neck hole

Cast off 9 stitches

Cast on 6 stitches

16 rows (body)

15 stitches   15 stitches

34 rows (legs)

Cast off   Cast off

61

Doll

To knit the second leg, put the stitches from the safety pin onto your needle.

Make sure that you have the point of the needle towards the centre of the doll. You have to start with a new piece of yarn which you tie onto the first stitch.

Knit 34 rows (17 rows of bumps). This completes the second leg.

Cast off.

Sewing up

HEAD: Cut out a 4 inch (10 cms) diameter circle of t-shirt material. Pull this circle of material up around enough stuffing to make the right size head for your doll. Tie some thread around the head to keep it together.

FEET: Cut 2, 2$\frac{1}{2}$ inch (6 cms) circles of T-shirt material and, using the stuffing, make 2 feet as you made the head.

HANDS: Cut 2, 2 inch (5 cms) circles and make the hands.

LEGS: Fold the first leg in half lengthwise. Sew up the inside seam of the leg leaving the end open for the foot. Pack the extra material of the foot into the bottom of the leg and sew it in. Sew the other leg the same way. Stuff the legs firmly.

ARMS: Fold over the arms. Sew the cast on and cast off edges together. This makes an arm seam that is underneath the arm. Sew in the hands as you did the feet. Stuff the arms just to the armpits - don't do the chest area yet.

HEAD: Push the extra material of the head into the neck hole and sew in. Sew the centre back seam.

BODY: Stuff the body. Sew up the last seam across the upper back.

HAIR: Sew the hair. We used coloured fleece which we sewed onto her head where she parts her hair. We then tied her hair in 2 pony tails at the neck.

EYES and MOUTH: You can either make eyes and mouth with coloured pens, or you can use embroidery thread to sew on the eyes and mouth.

Horse

6mm (US g10) needles, 2 balls 50 gram 'chunky' weight yarn, fleece for stuffing, thin thread for eyes, different coloured yarn for the mane, sewing up needle or bodkin.

(This horse can be made smaller by using thinner needles and thinner yarn).

The horse is made from two identical pieces that are sewn together. You will follow the instructions below twice to make the two pieces.

You start knitting at the bottom of one of the horse's legs.

Cast on 10 stitches.

Knit 28 rows (14 rows of bumps). Cut the yarn leaving a hand's length piece.

Slip this completed leg to the knob end of your needle and leave it there while you knit the second leg.

On this same needle that has the first leg pushed up to the knob, cast on 10 stitches for the second leg.

Knit 28 rows (14 rows of bumps).

Now you will connect the two legs to the body by knitting them all together.

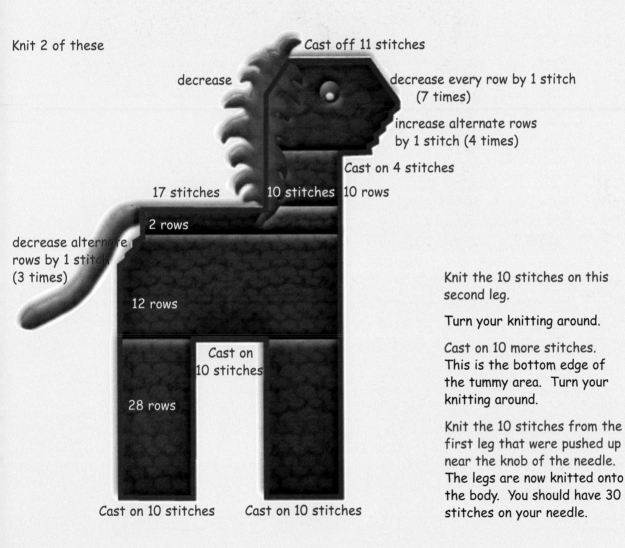

Knit 2 of these

Cast off 11 stitches

decrease

decrease every row by 1 stitch
(7 times)

increase alternate rows
by 1 stitch (4 times)

Cast on 4 stitches

17 stitches

10 stitches 10 rows

2 rows

decrease alternate
rows by 1 stitch
(3 times)

12 rows

Cast on
10 stitches

28 rows

Cast on 10 stitches

Cast on 10 stitches

Knit the 10 stitches on this second leg.

Turn your knitting around.

Cast on 10 more stitches. This is the bottom edge of the tummy area. Turn your knitting around.

Knit the 10 stitches from the first leg that were pushed up near the knob of the needle. The legs are now knitted onto the body. You should have 30 stitches on your needle.

Horse

Knit 12 rows (6 rows of bumps).

Now you start decreasing to make the rounded rear end of the horse.

At the beginning of the next 3 alternate rows decrease 1 stitch by knitting 2 stitches together. Alternate rows means every other row, so you decrease on one row and knit one row plain.

You should now have 27 stitches on your needle.

Knit 2 rows.

Cast off 17 stitches. This is the top edge of the back.
Knit the last 9 stitches in this row.

Knit 10 rows. This is the neck.

At the beginning of this row cast on 4 stitches and finish this row.
This is the bottom of the head.

Knit 1 row.

At the beginning of the next 4 alternate rows cast on 1 stitch. Alternate rows means every other row, so you increase on one row and knit one row plain.

You should now have 18 stitches on your needle and have knitted 8 rows (4 rows of bumps). This is the horse's nose.

At the beginning of each of the next 7 rows decrease 1 stitch.

Cast off the 11 remaining stitches.

Knit a second piece exactly like this first one.

EARS:

Cast on 6 stitches.

Knit 3 rows.

At the beginning of each of the next 5 rows decrease 1 stitch.

Pull the needle out of the last stitch, put the yarn through the stitch and pull it up.

8 rows

Cast on 6 stitches

Horse

Sewing up

LEGS: Sew the 4 legs up first. Fold eachleg in half lengthwise. Make small in and out stitches along the cast on edge (the bottom of the foot). Gently pull this in so it forms a small circle. Sew up the inside seam of the leg. Sew this seam tightly with small stitches so the leg will not stretch out of shape.

Note: Make sure you fold the 2 legs on the same piece of the horse the same way. If you do this then the inside seams will both be facing the same way.

Also, make sure that on the second piece of the horse you fold the legs in the opposite direction, so that when you put the two halves together the inside seams of the legs will be facing each other.

Stuff the legs firmly.

BODY: Put the two halves of the horse together with the inside seams of the legs towards each other.

Sew the top of the back seam, the rear end seam, the belly seam and the chest seam as far as the base of the neck.

Stuff and shape the body.

HEAD: Sew the head together, starting at the chin, working around the head to the back of the neck.

Stuff and shape the head and neck.

Sew the last seam, which is the front of the neck seam.

TAIL: Finger knit a tail using 4 strands of yarn. Leave the ends long for the very end of the tail. Sew the tail on.

EARS: Sew the ears on in the proper spot, folding them in a little as you do so.

Use the loop and lock stitch to create a mane (see page 51).

Use thin thread to make the eyes.

Purl stitch

The purl stitch is not very different from the knit stitch. You still hold your needle with the stitches on it in your left hand and the empty needle you hold in your right hand. You will use your right hand to move the yarn. You will make new stitches from the stitches on your left hand needle as you move those stitches over to your right hand needle.

Purl stitch verse

In front of the fence,
Catch the goat,
Back we go,
Jump off the boat.

You will notice that you go in under the fence in the opposite direction from the way you go

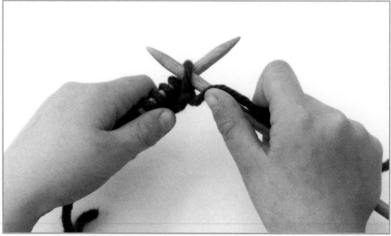

In front of the fence,

Catch the goat,

70

Back we go,

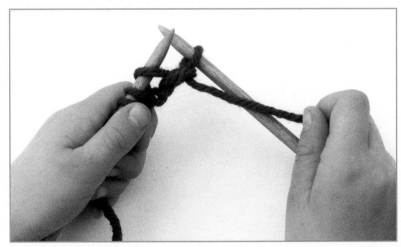

Jump off the boat.

under the fence for the knit stitch.

When catching your goat make sure that your yarn goes from top to bottom.

Back we go is opposite to back we come that you did for the knit stitch.

You are pulling your goat back under the fence away from you, whereas when you do the knit stitch you are pulling your sheep back under the fence towards you.

Jump off the boat is the same as off we leap. In both these moves you are taking an old stitch off the left hand needle so your new stitch will be free on the right hand needle.

Purl stitch

The other difference about a purl stitch is that the yarn starts and finishes at the front of the knitting – the side of the knitting towards you. In a knit stitch the yarn always starts and finishes at the back of the knitting – the side of the knitting away from you.

A purl stitch is really like a reverse knit stitch. The finished stitch has the bump on the front instead of on the back like the knit stitch has.

If you knit row after row of purl stitch, the fabric you knit will look exactly the same as fabric made by knitting row after row of knit stitch. They will both have rows of bumps. They are both called garter stitch.

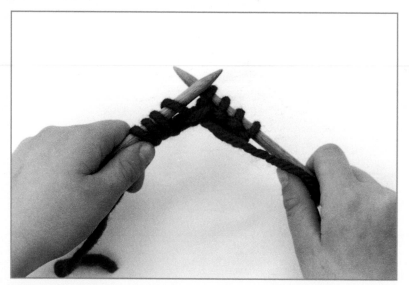

4 stitches purled. Notice the bumps are at the front and the yarn comes out of the front.

Stocking stitch

If you work one row in knit stitch (knit one row) and work one row in purl stitch (purl one row), all the bumps will be on one side and the other side will be smooth. This is called stocking stitch. Using the same thickness of yarn, the fabric that you make using stocking stitch is thinner and more flexible than the fabric you make using garter stitch. This stitch is used to make all sorts of clothing.

Can you count 8 rows of stocking stitch? The stitches of row 9 are sitting on the needle.

Ribbing

If you work one stitch in knit and one stitch in purl you will make a fabric that has up and down rows of smooth and bumps. This is called ribbing. It is sturdy and will not curl up. It is also quite stretchy. Because of these qualities it is used to make bands at the beginning and ending of many types of clothing. You can make ribbing that is knit 2, purl 2, as shown here, or any combination of knit and purl stitches.

The difficult thing about working ribbing is that you have to change the yarn from the back to the front of the fabric, when you change from doing a knit stitch to a purl stitch. When you change from a purl stitch to a knit stitch you must change the yarn from the front of the fabric to the back of the fabric. You really have to pay attention when you are working ribbing!

Purl stitch problems –
where they occur and how to correct them

A mistake in stocking stitch

This shows stocking stitch done incorrectly. Someone did a row of purl where they should have been doing knit stitch, or vice versa.

Take your knitting out row by row to before the mistake. Remember, when you are working in stocking stitch, all the bumps are on the same side. If you want the bumps to be away from you, you must do a row of knit stitches. If you want the bumps to be towards you, you must do a row of purl stitches.

Mistakes in ribbing

This shows 2 x 2 ribbing done incorrectly. Someone got their knit and purl stitches mixed up.

Take the knitting out row by row, if there is a whole row that is wrong, to before the mistake. Take your time and pay close attention when you are doing the ribbing. Remember, when you do this correctly, you should have up and down rows of bumps and smooth.

Purl stitch problems

If you forget to change the yarn from the back to the front when you are changing from a knit stitch to a purl stitch, you will create a new stitch and mess up your ribbing something terrible!

The same is true if you forget to change the yarn from the front to the back when you are changing from a purl stitch to a knit stitch.

Take the ribbing out row by row to correct this mistake. Work very slowly and remember to change the yarn when you change from a knit stitch to a purl stitch or from a purl stitch to a knit stitch.

Can you see the extra stitch (the ninth from the right) ?

Projects using
knit stitch and purl stitch

Cat

6mm (US g10) needles, a small quantity 'chunky' weight yarn, fleece for stuffing, thin thread for eyes, yarn for whiskers, sewing up needle or bodkin.

(This cat can be made smaller by using thinner needles and thinner yarn).

You start knitting at the bottom of the cat.

Cast on 18 stitches.

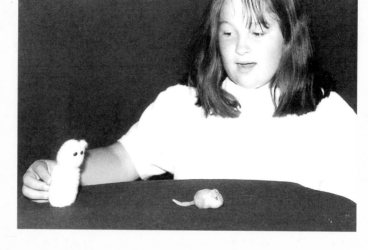

Knit 20 rows (10 rows of bumps). This is the body. This is garter stitch and looks 'bumpy'.

Now do 10 rows of stocking stitch. Remember that this is knit 1 row, purl 1 row.
This will be smooth on the right side and bumpy on the wrong side. This is the head.

Cast off.

Cast off 18 stitches

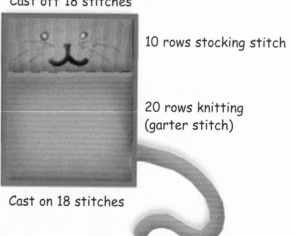

10 rows stocking stitch

20 rows knitting
(garter stitch)

Cast on 18 stitches

78

Sewing up

BODY: Fold your cat in half lengthwise.

The seam will be on one side of the cat.

Make small in and out stitches along the cast on edge – the bottom of the cat.

Pull the yarn up so the bottom forms a circle.

Sew up the side seam.

Stuff.

HEAD: Sew along the top of the head.

Using thin thread make a few stitches to form the ears at the corners of the head.

Using thin thread again, make in and out stitches around the neck. Pull up to form the neck.

Tie on a ribbon.

TAIL: Finger knit a tail and sew it on.

You can either give your cat whiskers and eyes or leave it plain.

Chicken

4mm (US g6) needles, a small quantity 'double knitting' weight yarn, felt for the comb and beak, thin thread for eyes, sewing up needle or bodkin, cardboard for making the pom-pom.

(This project does not work well with thicker needles and yarn).

This project is fun because you can use it as either an egg warmer or a toy.

You start knitting at the bottom of the chicken.

Cast on 32 stitches.

Work 10 rows of 2 x 2 ribbing. This is where you knit 2 stitches, then purl two stitches, all the way across the row. You will end with 2 purl stitches, so when you turn your knitting around you are ready to start again with 2 knit stitches.

Knit 14 rows (7 rows of bumps). This is the body.

At the beginning of each of the next 2 rows cast off 10 stitches. This is the top of the back. You should now have 12 stitches on your needle.

Knit 8 rows (4 rows of bumps). This is the head.

Cast off.

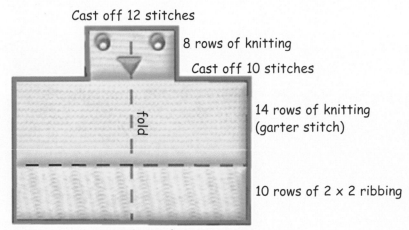

Cast off 12 stitches

8 rows of knitting

Cast off 10 stitches

14 rows of knitting (garter stitch)

fold

10 rows of 2 x 2 ribbing

Cast on 32 stitches

80

Sewing up

BODY: Fold the chicken in half with the two side seams together. They make the tail area of the chicken. Sew up the tail side, along the back and over the head.

COMB and BEAK: Make a comb and beak of red felt. Using red thread, sew them onto your chicken.

TAIL: Make a pom-pom tail and sew this on - see following page.

Making a pom-pom

To make a pom-pom, cut 2, 1 inch (2 ¹/₂ cm) diameter round pieces of cardboard. Cut half inch (1 ¹/₄ cm) holes in the centres. Using the two pieces of cardboard as one, tape one end of a piece of yarn to the cardboard, using the colour you would like for your chicken's tail. Start winding the yarn through the centre of this cardboard doughnut and around the outside. Go all the way around the doughnut so you end up with a yarn doughnut. After a while it becomes difficult to get the yarn through in the middle of the doughnut. You can thread your yarn on a darning needle and put it through that way. The more yarn you have in your doughnut the nicer your pom-pom will look.

Now hold the doughnut carefully so it doesn't fall apart when you do this next step. Putting your scissors in between the two pieces of cardboard, cut the yarn all the way round the outer edge of the doughnut. Tie a double piece of yarn very tightly between the 2 pieces of cardboard and around the short pieces of yarn. Take off the cardboard circles. The short pieces of yarn will now fluff out to make the pom-pom. You can trim off any pieces that are too long.

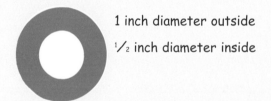

1 inch diameter outside

¹/₂ inch diameter inside

Mother Sea Otter

4mm (US g6) needles, 1 ball 50 gram 'double knitting' weight yarn, fleece for stuffing, thin thread for eyes and nose, sewing up needle or bodkin.

(This project does not work well with thicker needles and yarn).

This project is worked in stocking stitch so we use the phrase 'work 2 rows' instead of 'knit 2 rows' because you will knit 1 row and purl 1 row. Because this is a complicated pattern, mark the rows with a pencil as you complete them. That way you won't get lost.

You start knitting at the tail.

Cast on 6 stitches.

Beginning with a knit row, work 4 rows.

At the beginning of each of the next 2 rows cast on 1 stitch.

Work 4 rows.

At the beginning of each of the next 2 rows cast on 1 stitch.

Work 4 rows.

At the beginning of each of the next 2 rows cast on 1 stitch.
You should now have 12 stitches on your needle.
You have now finished the tail and are starting on the body.

At the beginning of each of the next 6 rows cast on 1 stitch.

Work 2 rows.

At the beginning of each of the next 8 rows cast on 1 stitch.

Work 6 rows. This is the fat tummy area.

At the beginning of each of the next 2 rows decrease 1 stitch. On a knit row, to

Mother Sea Otter

decrease you knit 2 together. On a purl row, to decrease you purl 2 together.

Work 2 rows.

At the beginning of each of the next 2 rows decrease 1 stitch.

Work 2 rows.

At the beginning of each of the next 2 rows decrease 1 stitch. This is the armpit area. You should now have 20 stitches left on your needle.

At the beginning of each of the next 2 rows cast on 1 stitch.

At the beginning of each of the next 2 rows cast on 2 stitches.

At the beginning of each of the next 4 rows cast on 3 stitches. You should now have 38 stitches on your needle. These are the arms.

Work 4 rows.

At the beginning of each of the next 4 rows cast off 4 stitches. This is the front edge of the front arms and paws. It is shorter in length than the back edge so that when they are sewn together the

Cast off 6 stitches

2 centre stitches

Cast on 6 stitches

arms will curve in. You should now have 22 stitches left on your needle.

Work 2 rows. This is the neck.

Mark the centre 2 stitches with a piece of different coloured yarn. The head shape is made just the way the pig's head shape was made, except there was only 1 centre stitch in that pattern.

In each of the next 6 rows decrease 1 on either side of the centre 2 stitches. Remember, to decrease 1 stitch in a knit row you knit 2 together, and in a purl row you purl 2 together. You should now have 10 stitches left on your needle.

Work 1 row without decreasing.

Work 1 row decreasing 1 stitch either side of the 2 centre stitches.

Work 1 row without decreasing.

Work 1 row decreasing 1 stitch either side of the 2 centre stitches. You should now have 6 stitches left on your needle.

Cast off.

Mother Sea Otter

Sewing up

TAIL: Sew the tail up first. Make small in and out stitches along the cast on edge and pull into a circle to form the end of the tail. Sew up the tail seam.

Stuff and shape with your hands.

ARMS: Now sew each arm up. Make small in and out stitches at the end of the paw and pull into a circle. Sew up the arm seam. The lower arm seam is longer than the upper arm seam, so pin the two arm seams together at the armpit, and spread the extra length of the lower arm seam out evenly along the upper arm seam. Sew together.

Stuff and shape with your hands. The arms should be curving in because of the way you sewed up the arm seam.

BODY: Fold the sea otter in half lengthwise and sew up the tummy seam to the armpits.

Stuff and shape.

HEAD: Now sew up the head. Make small in and out stitches along the cast off edge and pull them into a circle to make the nose. Fold the head in half lengthwise and sew the seam up, pulling the yarn tightly after each stitch so her head is pulled forward, and she can see to crack shellfish on her belly. Leave a little space by the arms to stuff the head, neck and chest, and after stuffing sew up this last little seam.

Shape the head. Use black yarn to make a nose.

Baby Sea Otter

The Baby Sea Otter pattern is very similar to the Mother Sea Otter pattern except it is not as fat proportionally and its arms are smaller. We did not include this pattern as we thought you would enjoy the challenge of working it out yourself.

Boy with hands in his pockets

4mm (US g6) needles, small quantities of various colours 'double knitting' weight yarn, fleece for stuffing, thin thread for eyes and mouth, sewing up needle or bodkin.

(This project does not work well with thicker needles and yarn).

It is worked mostly in stocking stitch – knit 1 row, purl 1 row.
You will need different colours of yarn to make the shoes, trousers, shirt, face and hat.

You start knitting at the boy's feet.

Cast on 16 stitches.

Work 4 rows, beginning with a knit row, in the colour for the shoes.

Change to trouser colour.

Work 10 rows, beginning with a knit row.

Boy with hands in his pockets

To make the tummy:

Knit 6 stitches, increase 1 stitch between each of the next 4 stitches, knit remaining 6 stitches.

You should now have 20 stitches on your needle. To increase in the middle of a row, pick up the bar of thread that lies between the needles, put it on to the left hand needle and knit into the back of it.

Purl 1 row.

Change to sweater colour.

Work 8 rows., beginning with a knit row.

Change to face colour.

Work 7 rows, beginning with a knit row.

Change to hat colour.

Knit 3 rows.

Next row, knit 2 together, knit 1, all across the row.

Knit 1 row.

Nest row, knit 2 together all across the row.

Break off a hand's length of yarn. Thread this through the remaining stitches instead of casting off. Pull out the needle and leave this part until last, to finish.

3 rows - hat

6 rows - face

8 rows - sweater

12 rows - trousers

4 rows - shoes

Cast on 16 stitches

Sewing up

LEGS, BODY and HEAD: Fold knitting in half lengthwise and sew up. With the seam in the middle of the back, sew across the bottom of the feet.

Stuff with fleece or other stuffing, then finish the top of the hat by pulling the stitches on the yarn into a circle and end with a locking stitch.

Run a thread through the lowest row of the face. Pull tight to make a neck.

Sew some stitches to make legs appear, remembering to use the same colour yarn as the trousers.

Sew some stitches at the side to make arms appear.

Sew some stitches around and under the hat, for hair.

Make some eyes with thin thread.

Finger knit a scarf.

Girl with hands in her pockets

To make the Girl with hands in her pockets follow the pattern for the boy and add a skirt.

Skirt pattern

The skirt is worked mostly in stocking stitch (knit 1 row, purl 1 row).

Start at the bottom of the skirt.

Cast on 28 stitches.

Knit 1 row.

Work 6 rows (start with a knit row).

At the beginning and end of the next row knit 2 together.
You will have 26 stitches left on your needle.

Purl 1 row.

At the beginning and end of the next row knit 2 together.
You will have 24 stitches left on your needle.

Purl 1 row.

Knit or purl 2 stitches together at the beginning and end of the next two rows. You will have 20 stitches left on your needle.

Cast off.

Fold the skirt so that the two side seams are together and the wrong side (purl) is facing in.
Start at the bottom of this seam with a locking stitch and oversew about half the way up.
Slip the skirt on the girl. Finish sewing up this back seam. End with a locking stitch.

She can wear her skirt long or roll it up once to make it shorter.

Making your own wooden knitting needles

To make the large wooden knitting needles shown below you will need 3/8 inch (1 cm) dowelling. This makes needles that are 6mm (US g10) size. Dowelling is often sold in 4 foot (1.2 metre) lengths, which is sufficient to make two pairs of needles. Measure the dowelling into 4 lengths, each 1 foot (30 cm) long and mark the lengths with a pencil. You will need either a vice or a helper to hold the dowelling while you saw. Unless you are really experienced with using a hand saw, it would be best to ask for help from an adult, as saws are very sharp.

When you have your 4 pieces of dowelling cut, you need to make one end of each piece

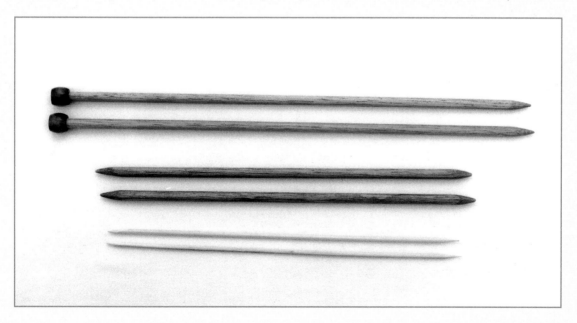

Making your own wooden knitting needles

pointed. You could whittle the ends with a sharp knife, but here again an adult's help is essential. You could sand them with a very coarse sandpaper, but this takes a very long time. We have found that the point can be made by sharpening each piece in a pencil sharpener.

Once the points are made, you are ready to sand the points and needles so they will be very, very smooth. Start with a rougher grade of sand paper, for example 50, if the points have very rough spots in them. Don't make the ends too pointed. Finish with a finer grade of sand paper, for example 180. Remember, the smoother your needles are the easier they will be to work with.

Now you need to make ends for your needles. We used wooden beads and glued them on.

You can either leave your needles plain or finish them in one of the following ways: We recommend an oil finish followed by satin wax, available from hardware stores, but for this method you will need the help of an adult. Alternatively, you can finish the needles yourself by applying a thin film of vegetable oil onto the sanded needles, and rubbing it in thoroughly, then polishing well with a soft cloth.

The smaller wooden needles are double ended needles. They are made from bamboo skewers that you buy in the grocery store. You can buy a package of 50 skewers for very little money. Cut each skewer in half. Sand on a point and sand the needle smooth.

These needles are a lot of fun to use after you have learned the basics of knitting. You can make little, tiny replicas of everything, and you can use any thin yarn; 2 ply yarn and crochet cotton are nice to work with.

Bibliography

Editors of American Fabric and Fashion Magazine. The New Encyclopedia of Textiles, 3rd Edition, Prentice Hall Inc., Englewood Cliffs, New Jersey, U.S.A., 1980.

Harvey, Michael, Patons – A Story of Hand-knitting, Springwood Books Limited, Great Britain, 1985.

Thomas, Mary, Mary Thomas's Knitting Book, Dover Publications, New York, U.S.A., 1972.

Taylor, Gertrude, America's Knitting Book, Charles Scribner's Sons, New York, U.S.A., 1968.

By the same authors

Knitting for Children – A second book by Bonnie Gosse and Jill Allerton building on the success of A First Book of Knitting for Children.

In this second book, the authors bring many new skills and a wider variety of patterns to make. These include a variety of clothes patterns, from baby 'running' shoes up to hats, together with animals, and dolls with clothing. The patterns are all given with clear instructions and accompanied by artistic photographs, suitable for both children and adults to make.

108 pages with numerous colour illustrations.

Published by Wynstones Press 2002. ISBN 9780946206 53 7.

Biographies

The inspiration for this book came from the students of the Vancouver Waldorf School. For them, completion of a handwork project always brings joy and great satisfaction.

Jill Allerton learned to knit when she was 3 years old! Now a grandmother of 7, and a long time teacher of handwork at the Vancouver Waldorf School, she has taught hundreds of children the joy of knitting and sewing.

Bonnie Gosse has always loved to create handicrafts of many kinds. Her book with husband Dave Gosse "Soapstone Carving for Children" (ISBN 0 921254318) has introduced the magic of soapstone carving to many children and adults. Her successful environmental board game "Keep it Green" has helped people in many countries to know how to live in balance with their environment.

Dave Gosse   Rebecca Gosse   Bryan Anderson
Bonnie Gosse   Sylvie Gosse   Jill Allerton

Wynstones Press

Wynstones Press publishes a range of books, mostly for children, parents and teachers. These include childrens' picture books, childrens' fiction and resource books.
The resource books cover a variety of subject areas, including knitting, poems, songs and stories for young children, pentatonic music and a volume on ancient mythologies.

Also available is a wide selection of postcards, folded cards and prints reproduced from original work by a variety of different artists.

Wynstones Press distributes a selection of Advent Calendars.

For further information please contact:

Wynstones Press
Ruskin Glass Centre
Wollaston Road
Stourbridge DY8 4HE. England.

Telephone: +44 (0) 1384 399455
Email: info@wynstonespress.com
Website: wynstonespress.com